The Story of Frithiof

Anonymous

Alpha Editions

This edition published in 2024

ISBN : 9789362922779

Design and Setting By
Alpha Editions
www.alphaedis.com
Email - info@alphaedis.com

As per information held with us this book is in Public Domain.
This book is a reproduction of an important historical work. Alpha Editions uses the best technology to reproduce historical work in the same manner it was first published to preserve its original nature. Any marks or number seen are left intentionally to preserve its true form.

Contents

CHAPTER I. Of King Belt and Thorstein Vikingson and their Children.................................- 1 -

CHAPTER II. Frithiof wooeth Ingibiorg of those Brethren.......................................- 3 -

CHAPTER III. Of King Ring and those Brethren...- 5 -

CHAPTER IV. Frithiof goes to Baldur's Meads..- 7 -

CHAPTER V. Those Brethren come Home again. ....- 8 -

CHAPTER VI. Frithiof Sails for the Orkneys..- 10 -

CHAPTER VII. Frithiof at the Orkneys. ....- 18 -

CHAPTER VIII. King Ring weddeth Ingibiorg...- 21 -

CHAPTER IX. Frithiof brings the Tribute to the Kings. ....- 22 -

CHAPTER X. Frithiof made an Outlaw. ....- 25 -

CHAPTER XI. Frithiof fareth to see King Ring and Ingibiorg. ....- 27 -

CHAPTER XII. Frithiof saves the King and Queen on the Ice..- 31 -

CHAPTER XIII. The King sleeps before Frithiof. ....- 32 -

CHAPTER XIV. King Ring's Gift to Frithiof. ....- 33 -

CHAPTER XV. Frithiof King in Sogn. ....- 36 -

CHAPTER I.
Of King Beli and Thorstein Vikingson and their Children.

Thus beginneth the tale, telling how that King Beli ruled over Sogn-land; three children had he, whereof Helgi was his first son, and Halfdan his second, but Ingibiorg his daughter. Ingibiorg was fair of face and wise of mind, and she was ever accounted the foremost of the king's children.

Now a certain strand went west of the firth, and a great stead was thereon, which was called Baldur's Meads; a Place of Peace was there, and a great temple, and round about it a great garth of pales: many gods were there, but amidst them all was Baldur held of most account. So jealous were the heathen men of this stead, that they would have no hurt done therein to man nor beast, nor might any man have dealings with a woman there.

Sowstrand was the name of that stead whereas the king dwelt; but on the other side the firth was an abode named Foreness, where dwelt a man called Thorstein, the son of Viking; and his stead was over against the king's dwelling.

Thorstein had a son by his wife called Frithiof: he was the tallest and strongest of men, and more furnished of all prowess than any other man, even from his youth up. Frithiof the Bold was he called, and so well beloved was he, that all prayed for good things for him.

Now the king's children were but young when their mother died; but a goodman of Sogn, named Hilding, prayed to have the king's daughter to foster: so there was she reared well and needfully: and she was called Ingibiorg the Fair. Frithiof also was fostered of goodman Hilding, wherefore was he foster-brother to the king's daughter, and they two were peerless among children.

Now King Beli's chattels began to ebb fast away from his hands, for he was grown old.

Thorstein had rule over the third part of the realm, and in him lay the king's greatest strength.

Every third year Thorstein feasted the king at exceeding great cost, and the king feasted Thorstein the two years between.

Helgi, Beli's son, from his youth up turned much to blood-offering: neither were those brethren well-beloved.

Thorstein had a ship called Ellidi, which pulled fifteen oars on either board; it ran up high stem and stern, and was strong-built like an ocean-going ship, and its bulwarks were clamped with iron.

So strong was Frithiof that he pulled the two bow oars of Ellidi; but either oar was thirteen ells long, and two men pulled every oar otherwise.

Frithiof was deemed peerless amid the young men of that time, and the king's sons envied him, whereas he was more praised than they.

Now King Beli fell sick; and when the sickness lay heavy on him he called his sons to him and said to them: "This sickness will bring me to mine end, therefore will I bid you this, that ye hold fast to those old friends that I have had; for meseems in all things ye fall short of that father and son, Thorstein and Frithiof, yea, both in good counsel and in hardihood. A mound ye shall raise over me."

So with that Beli died.

Thereafter Thorstein fell sick; so he spake to Frithiof: "Kinsman," says he, "I will crave this of thee, that thou bow thy will before the king's sons, for their dignity's sake; yet doth my heart speak goodly things to me concerning thy fortune. Now would I be laid in my mound over against King Beli's mound, down by the sea on this side the firth, whereas it may be easiest for us to cry out each to each of tidings drawing nigh."

A little after this Thorstein departed, and was laid in mound even as he had bidden; but Frithiof took the land and chattels after him. Biorn and Asmund were Frithiof's foster-brethren; they were big and strong men both.

CHAPTER II.
Frithiof wooeth Ingibiorg of those Brethren.

So Frithiof became the most famed of men, and the bravest in all things that may try a man.

Biorn, his foster-brother, he held in most account of all, but Asmund served the twain of them.

The ship Ellidi, he gat, the best of good things, of his father's heritage, and another possession therewith—a gold ring; no dearer was in Norway.

So bounteous a man was Frithiof withal, that it was the talk of most, that he was a man of no less honour than those brethren, but it were for the name of king; and for this cause they held Frithiof in hate and enmity, and it was a heavy thing to them that he was called greater than they: furthermore they thought they could see that Ingibiorg, their sister, and Frithiof were of one mind together.

It befell hereon that the kings had to go to a feast to Frithiof s house at Foreness; and there it happened according to wont that he gave to all men beyond that they were worthy of. Now Ingibiorg was there, and she and Frithiof talked long together; and the king's daughter said to him:—

"A goodly gold ring hast thou."

"Yea, in good sooth," said he.

Thereafter went those brethren to their own home, and greater grew their enmity of Frithiof.

A little after grew Frithiof heavy of mood, and Biorn, his foster-brother, asked him why he fared so.

He said he had it in his mind to woo Ingibiorg. "For though I be named by a lesser name than those brethren, yet am I not fashioned lesser."

"Even so let us do then," quoth Biorn. So Frithiof fared with certain men unto those brethren; and the kings were sitting on their father's mound when Frithiof greeted them well, and then set forth his wooing, and prayed for their sister Ingibiorg, the daughter of Beli.

The kings said: "Not overwise is this thine asking, whereas thou wouldst have us give her to one who lacketh dignity; wherefore we gainsay thee this utterly."

Said Frithiof: "Then is mine errand soon sped; but in return never will I give help to you henceforward, nay, though ye need it ever so much."

They said they heeded it nought: so Frithiof went home, and was joyous once more.

CHAPTER III.
Of King Ring and those Brethren.

There was a king named Ring, who ruled over Ringrealm, which also was in Norway: a mighty folk-king he was, and a great man, but come by now unto his latter days.

Now he spake to his men: "Lo, I have heard that the sons of King Beli have brought to nought their friendship with Frithiof, who is the noblest of men; wherefore will I send men to these kings, and bid them choose whether they will submit them to me and pay me tribute, or else that I bring war on them: and all things then shall lie ready to my hand to take, for they have neither might nor wisdom to withstand me; yet great fame were it to my old age to overcome them."

After that fared the messengers of King Ring, and found those brethren, Helgi and Halfdan, in Sogn, and spake to them thus: "King Ring sends bidding to you to send him tribute, or else will he war against your realm."

They answered and said that they would not learn in the days of their youth what they would be loth to know in their old age, even how to serve King Ring with shame. "Nay, now shall we draw together all the folk that we may."

Even so they did; but now, when they beheld their force that it was but little, they sent Hilding their fosterer to Frithiof to bid him come help them against King Ring. Now Frithiof sat at the knave-play when Hilding came thither, who spake thus: "Our kings send thee greeting, Frithiof, and would have thy help in battle against King Ring, who cometh against their realm with violence and wrong."

Frithiof answered him nought, but said to Biorn, with whom he was playing: "A bare place in thy board, foster-brother, and nowise mayst thou amend it; nay, for my part I shall beset thy red piece there, and wot whether it be safe."

Then Hilding spake again:

"King Helgi bade me say thus much, Frithiof, that thou shouldst go on this journey with them, or else look for ill at their hands when they at the last come back."

"A double game, foster-brother," said Biorn; "and two ways to meet thy play."

Frithiof said: "Thy play is to fall first on the knave, yet the double game is sure to be."

No other outcome of his errand had Hilding: he went back speedily to the kings, and told them Frithiof's answer.

They asked Hilding what he made out of those words. He said:

"Whereas he spake of the bare place he will have been thinking of the lack in this journey of yours; but when he said he would beset the red piece, that will mean Ingibiorg, your sister; so give ye all the heed ye may to her. But whereas I threatened him with ill from you, Biorn deemed the game a double one; but Frithiof said that the knave must be set on first, speaking thereby of King Ring."

So then the brethren arrayed them for departing; but, ere they went, they let bring Ingibiorg and eight women with her to Baldur's Meads, saying that Frithiof would not be so mad rash as to go see her thither, since there was none who durst make riot there.

Then fared those brethren south to Jadar, and met King Ring in Sogn-Sound.

Now, herewith was King Ring most of all wroth that the brothers had said that they accounted it a shame to fight with a man so old that he might not get a-horseback unholpen.

CHAPTER IV.
Frithiof goes to Baldur's Meads.

Straightway whenas the kings were gone away Frithiof took his raiment of state and set the goodly gold ring on his arm; then went the foster-brethren down to the sea and launched Ellidi. Then said Biorn: "Whither away, foster-brother?"

"To Baldur's Meads," said Frithiof, "to be glad with Ingibiorg.",

Biorn said: "A thing unmeet to do, to make the gods wroth with us."

"Well, it shall be risked this time," said Frithiof; "and withal, more to me is Ingibiorg's grace than Baldur's grame."

Therewith they rowed over the firth, and went up to Baldur's Meads and to Ingibiorg's bower, and there she sat with eight maidens, and the new comers were eight also.

But when they came there, lo, all the place was hung with cloth of pall and precious webs.

Then Ingibiorg arose and said:

"Why art thou so overbold, Frithiof, that thou art come here without the leave of my brethren to make the gods angry with thee?"

Frithiof says: "Howsoever that may be, I hold thy love of more account than the gods' hate."

Ingibiorg answered: "Welcome art thou here, thou and thy men!"

Then she made place for him to sit beside her, and drank to him in the best of wine; and thus they sat and were merry together.

Then beheld Ingibiorg the goodly ring on his arm, and asked him if that precious thing were his own.

Frithiof said Yea, and she praised the ring much. Then Frithiof said:

"I will give thee the ring if thou wilt promise to give it to no one, but to send it to me when thou no longer shalt have will to keep it: and hereon shall we plight troth each to other."

So with this troth-plighting they exchanged rings.

Frithiof was oft at Baldur's Meads a-night time, and every day between whiles would he go thither to be glad with Ingibiorg.

CHAPTER V.
Those Brethren come Home again.

Now tells the tale of those brethren, that they met King Ring, and he had more folk than they: then went men betwixt them, and sought to make peace, so that no battle should be: thereto King Ring assented on such terms that the brethren should submit them to him, and give him in marriage Ingibiorg their sister, with the third part of all their possessions.

The kings said Yea thereto, for they saw that they had to do with overwhelming might: so the peace was fast bound by oaths, and the wedding was to be at Sogn whenas King Ring should go see his betrothed.

So those brethren fare home with their folk, right ill content with things. But Frithiof, when he deemed that the brethren might be looked for home again, spake to the king's daughter:

"Sweetly and well have ye done to us, neither has goodman Baldur been wroth with us; but now as soon as ye wot of the kings' coming home, spread the sheets of your beds abroad on the Hall of the Goddesses, for that is the highest of all the garth, and we may see it from our stead."

The king's daughter said: "Thou dost not after the like of any other: but certes, we welcome dear friends whenas ye come to us."

So Frithiof went home; and the next morning he went out early, and when he came in then he spake and sang:

> "Now must I tell
>
> To our good men
>
> That over and done
>
> Are our fair journeys;
>
> No more a-shipboard
>
> Shall we be going,
>
> For there are the sheets
>
> Spread out a-bleaching."

Then they went out, and saw that the Hall of the Goddesses was all thatched with white linen. Biorn spake and said: "Now are the kings come home, and but a little while have we to sit in peace, and good were it, meseems, to gather folk together."

So did they, and men came flocking thither.

Now the brethren soon heard of the ways of Frithiof and Ingibiorg, and of the gathering of men. So King Helgi spake:

"A wondrous thing how Baldur will bear what shame soever Frithiof and she will lay on him! Now will I send men to him, and wot what atonement he will offer us, or else will I drive him from the land, for our strength seemeth to me not enough that we should fight with him as now."

So Hilding, their fosterer, bare the king's errand to Frithiof and his friends, and spake in such wise: "This atonement the kings will have of thee, Frithiof, that thou go gather the tribute of the Orkneys, which has not been paid since Beli died, for they need money, whereas they are giving Ingibiorg their sister in marriage, and much of wealth with her."

Frithiof said: "This thing only somewhat urges us to peace, the good will of our kin departed; but no trustiness will those brethren show herein. But this condition I make, that our lands be in good peace while we are away." So this was promised and all bound by oaths.

Then Frithiof arrays him for departing, and is captain of men brave and of good help, eighteen in company.

Now his men asked him if he would not go to King Helgi and make peace with him, and pray himself free from Baldur's wrath.

But he answered: "Hereby I swear that I will never pray Helgi for peace."

Then he went aboard Ellidi, and they sailed out along the Sognnrth.

But when Frithiof was gone from home, King Halfdan spake to Helgi his brother: "Better lordship and more had we if Frithiof had payment for his masterful deed: now therefore let us burn his stead, and bring on him and his men such a storm on the sea as shall make an end of them."

Helgi said it was a thing meet to be done.

So then they burned up clean all the stead at Foreness and robbed it of all goods; and after that sent for two witch-wives, Heidi and Hamglom, and gave them money to raise against Frithiof and his men so mighty a storm that they should all be lost at sea. So they sped the witch-song, and went up on the witch-mount with spells and sorcery.

CHAPTER VI.
Frithiof Sails for the Orkneys.

SO when Frithiof and his men were come out of the Sognfirth there fell on them great wind and storm, and an exceeding heavy sea: but the ship drave on swiftly, for sharp built she was, and the best to breast the sea.

So now Frithiof sang:—

> "Oft let I swim from Sogn
>
> My tarred ship sooty-sided,
>
> When maids sat o'er the mead-horn
>
> Amidst of Baldur's Meadows;
>
> Now while the storm is wailing
>
> Farewell I bid you maidens,
>
> Still shall ye love us, sweet ones,
>
> Though Ellidi the sea fill."

Said Biorn: "Thou mightest well find other work to do than singing songs over the maids of Baldur's Meadows."

"Of such work shall I not speedily run dry, though," said Frithiof. Then they bore up north to the sounds nigh those isles that are called Solundir, and therewith was the gale at its hardest.

Then sang Frithiof:

> "Now is the sea a-swelling,
>
> And sweepeth the rack onward;
>
> Spells of old days cast o'er us
>
> Make ocean all unquiet;
>
> No more shall we be striving
>
> Mid storm with wash of billows,
>
> But Solundir shall shelter
>
> Our ship with ice-beat rock-walls."

So they lay to under the lee of the isles hight Solundir, and were minded to abide there; but straightway thereon the wind fell: then they turned away from under the lee of the islands, and now their voyage seemed hopeful to them, because the wind was fair awhile: but soon it began to freshen again.

Then sang Frithiof:

> "In days foredone
>
> From Foreness strand
>
> I rowed to meet
>
> Maid Ingibiorg;
>
> But now I sail
>
> Through chilly storm
>
> And wide away
>
> My long-worm driveth."

And now when they were come far out into the main, once more the sea waxed wondrous troubled, and a storm arose with so great drift of snow, that none might see the stem from the stern; and they shipped seas, so that they must be ever a-baling. So Frithiof sang:

> "The salt waves see we nought
>
> As seaward drive we ever
>
> Before the witch-wrought weather,
>
> We well-famed kings'-defenders:
>
> Here are we all a-standing,
>
> With all Solundir hull-down,
>
> Eighteen brave lads a-baling
>
> Black Ellidi to bring home."

Said Biorn: "Needs must he who fareth far fall in with diverse hap."

"Yea, certes, foster-brother," said Frithiof. And he sang withal:

> "Helgi it is that helpeth

> The white-head billows' waxing;
>
> Cold time unlike the kissing
>
> In the close of Baldut's Meadow!
>
> So is the hate of Helgi
>
> To that heart's love she giveth.
>
> O would that here I held her,
>
> Gift high above all giving!"

"Maybe," said Biorn, "she is looking higher than thou now art: what matter when all is said?"

"Well," says Frithiof, "now is the time to show ourselves to be men of avail, though blither tide it was at Baldur's Meadows."

So they turned to in manly wise, for there were the bravest of men come together in the best ship of the Northlands. But Frithiof sang a stave:

> "So come in the West-sea,
>
> Nought see I the billows,
>
> The sea-water seemeth
>
> As sweeping of wild-fire.
>
> Topple the rollers,
>
> Toss the hills swan-white,
>
> Ellidi wallows
>
> O'er steep of the wave-hills."

Then they shipped a huge sea, so that all stood a-baling. But Frithiof sang:

> "With love-moved mouth the maiden
>
> Mepledgeth though I founder.
>
> Ah! bright sheets lay a-bleaching,
>
> East there on brents the swan loves."

Biorn said: "Art thou of mind belike that the maids of Sogn will weep many tears over thee?"

Said Frithiof: "Surely that was in my mind."

Therewith so great a sea broke over the bows, that the water came in like the in-falling of a river; but it availed them much that the ship was so good, and the crew aboard her so hardy.

Now sang Biorn:

> "No widow, methinks,
>
> To thee or me drinks;
>
> No ring-bearer fair
>
> Biddeth draw near;
>
> Salt are our eyne
>
> Soaked in the brine;
>
> Strong our arms are no more,
>
> And our eyelids smart sore."

Quoth Asmund: "Small harm though your arms be tried somewhat, for no pity we had from you when we rubbed our eyes whenas ye must needs rise early a-mornings to go to Baldu's Meadows."

"Well," said Frithiof, "why singest thou not, Asmund?"

"Not I," said Asmund; yet sang a ditty straightway:

> "Sharp work about the sail was
>
> When o'er the ship seas tumbled,
>
> And there was I a-working
>
> Within-board 'gainst eight balers;
>
> Better it was to bower,
>
> Bringing the women breakfast,
>
> Than here to be 'mid billows
>
> Black Ellidi a-baling."

"Thou accountest thy help of no less worth than it is?" said Frithiof, laughing therewith; "but sure it showeth the thrall's blood in thee that thou wouldst fain be awaiting at table."

Now it blew harder and harder yet, so that to those who were aboard liker to huge peaks and mountains than to waves seemed the sea-breakers that crashed on all sides against the ship.

Then Frithiof sang:

> "On bolster I sat.
>
> In Baldur's Mead erst,
>
> And all songs that I could
>
> To the king's daughter sang;
>
> Now on Ran's bed belike
>
> Must I soon be a-lying,
>
> And another shall be
>
> By Ingibiorg's side."

Biorn said: "Great fear lieth ahead of us, foster-brother, and now dread hath crept into thy words, which is ill with such a good man as thou."

Says Frithiof: "Neither fear nor fainting is it, though I sing now of those our merry journeys; yet perchance more hath been said of them than need was: but most men would think death surer than life, if they were so bested as we be."

"Yet shall I answer thee somewhat," said Biorn, and sang:

> "Yet one gain have I gotten
>
> Thou gatst not 'mid thy fortune,
>
> For meet play did I make me
>
> With Ingibiorgs eight maidens;
>
> Red rings we laid together
>
> Aright in Baldur's Meadow,
>
> When far off was the warder
>
> Of the wide land of Halfdan."

"Well," said he, "we must be content with things as they are, foster-brother."

Therewith so great a sea smote them, that the bulwark was broken and both the sheets, and four men were washed overboard and all lost.

Then sang Frithiof:

> "Both sheets are bursten
>
> Amid the great billows,
>
> Four swains are sunk
>
> In the fathomless sea?

"Now, meseems," said Frithiof, "it may well be that some of us will go to the house of Ran, nor shall we deem us well sped if we come not thither in glorious array; wherefore it seems good to me that each man of us here should have somewhat of gold on him."

Then he smote asunder the ring, Ingibiorg's gift, and shared it between all his men, and sang a stave withal:

> "The red ring here I hew me
>
> Once owned of Halfdan's father,
>
> The wealthy lord of erewhile,
>
> Or the sea waves undo us,
>
> So on the guests shall gold be,
>
> If we have need of guesting;
>
> Meet so for mighty men-folk
>
> Amid Ran's hall to hold them."

"Not all so sure is it that we come there," said Biorn; "and yet it may well be so."

Now Frithiof and his folk found that the ship had great way on her, and they knew not what lay ahead, for all was mirk on either board, so that none might see the stem or stern from amidships; and therewith was there great drift of spray amid the furious wind, and frost, and snow, and deadly cold.

Now Frithiof went up to the masthead, and when he came down he said to his fellows: "A sight exceeding wondrous have I seen, for a great whale went in a ring about the ship, and I misdoubt me that we come nigh to some land, and that he is keeping the shore against us; for certes King Helgi has dealt with us in no friendly wise, neither will this his messenger be friendly. Moreover I saw two women on the back of the whale, and they it is who will have brought this great storm on us with the worst of spells and witchcraft; but now we shall try which may prevail, my fortune or their devilry, so steer ye at your straightest, and I will smite these evil things with beams."

Therewith he sang a stave:

"See I troll women

Twain on the billows,

Een they whom Helgi

Hither hath sent.

Ellidi now

Or ever her way stop

Shall smile the backs

Of these asunder."

So tells the tale that this wonder went with the good ship Ellidi, that she knew the speech of man.

But Biorn said: "Now may we see the treason of those brethren against us." Therewith he took the tiller, but Frithiof caught up a forked beam, and ran into the prow, and sang a stave:

"Ellidi, hail!

Leap high o'er the billows!

Break of the troll wives

Brow or teeth now!

Break cheek or jaw

Of the cursed woman,

One foot or twain

Of the ogress filthy."

Therewith he drave his fork at one of the skin-changers, and the beak of Ellidi smote the other on the back, and the backs of both were broken; but the whale took the deep, and gat him gone, and they never saw him after.

Then the wind fell, but the ship lay waterlogged; so Frithiof called out to his men, and bade bale out the ship, but Biorn said:

"No need to work now, verily!"

"Be thou not afeard, foster-brother," said Frithiof, "ever was it the wont of good men of old time to be helpful while they might, whatsoever should come after." And therewith he sang a stave:

> "No need, fairfellows,
>
> To fear the death-day;
>
> Rather be glad,
>
> Good men of mine:
>
> For if dreams wot aught
>
> All nights they say
>
> I yet shall have
>
> My Ingibiorg."

Then they baled out the ship; and they were now come nigh unto land; but there was yet a flaw of wind in their teeth. So then did Frithiof take the two bow oars again, and rowed full mightily. Therewith the weather brightened, and they saw that they were come out to Effia Sound, and so there they made land.

The crew were exceeding weary; but so stout a man was Frithiof that he bore eight men a-land over the foreshore, but Biorn bore two, and Asmund one. Then sang Frithiof:

> "Fast bare I up
>
> To the fire-lit house
>
> My men all dazed
>
> With the drift of the storm;
>
> And the sail moreover
>
> To the sand I carried;
>
> With the might of the sea
>
> Is there no more to do."

CHAPTER VII.
Frithiof at the Orkneys.

Now Earl Angantyr was at Effia whenas Frithiof and his folk came a-land there. But his way it was, when he was sitting at the drink, that one of his men should sit at the watch-window, looking weatherward from the drinking hall, and keep watch there. From a great horn drank he ever: and still as one was emptied another was filled for him. And he who held the watch when Frithiof came a-land was called Hallward; and now he saw where Frithiof and his men went, and sang a stave:

> "Men see I a-baling
>
> Amid the storm's might;
>
> Six bale on Ellidi
>
> Seven are a-rowing;
>
> Like is he in the stem,
>
> Straining hard at the oars,
>
> To Frithiof the bold,
>
> The brisk in the battle."

So when he had drunk out the horn, he cast it in through the window, and spake to the woman who gave him drink:

> "Take up from the floor,
>
> O fair-going woman,
>
> The horn cast adown
>
> Drunk out to the end!
>
> I behold men at sea
>
> Who, storm-beaten, shall need
>
> Help at our hands
>
> Ere the haven they make."

Now the Earl heard what Hallward sang; so he asked for tidings, and Hallward said: "Men are come a-land here, much forewearied, yet brave lads belike: but one of them is so hardy that he beareth the others. ashore."

Then said the Earl, "Go ye, and meet them, and welcome them in seemly wise; if this be Frithiof, the son of Hersir Thorstein, my friend, he is a man famed far and wide for all prowess."

Then there took up the word a man named Atli, a great viking, and he spake: "Now shall that be proven which is told of, that Frithiof hath sworn never to be first in the craving of peace."

There were ten men in company with him, all evil and outrageous, who often wrought berserksgang.

So when they met Frithiof they took to their weapons.

But Atli said:

"Good to turn hither, Frithiof! Clutching ernes should claw; and we no less, Frithiof! Yea, and now may'st thou hold to thy word, and not crave first for peace."

So Frithiof turned to meet them, and sang a stave:

> "Nay, nay, in nought
>
> Now shall ye cow us.
>
> Blenching hearts
>
> Isle-abiders!
>
> Alone with you ten
>
> The fight will I try,
>
> Rather than pray
>
> For peace at your hands."

Then came Hallward thereto, and spake: "The Earl wills that ye all be made welcome here: neither shall any set on you."

Frithiof said he would take that with a good heart; howsoever he was ready for either peace or war.

So thereon they went to the Earl, and he made Frithiof and all his men right welcome, and they abode with him, in great honour holden, through the wintertide; and oft would the Earl ask of their voyage: so Biorn sang:

"There baled we, wight fellows,

Washed over and over

On both boards

By billows;

For ten days we baled there,

And eight thereunto."

The Earl said: "Well nigh did the king undo you; it is ill seen of such-like kings as are meet for nought but to overcome men by wizardry. But now I wot," says Angantyr, "of thine errand hither, Frithiof, that thou art sent after the scat: whereto I give thee a speedy answer, that never shall King Helgi get scat of me, but to thee will I give money, even as much as thou wilt; and thou mayest call it scat if thou hast a mind to, or whatso else thou wilt."

So Frithiof said that he would take the money.

CHAPTER VIII.
King Ring weddeth Ingibiorg.

Now shall it be told of what came to pass in Norway the while Frithiof was away: for those brethren let burn up all the stead at Foreness. Moreover, while the weird sisters were at their spells they tumbled down from off their high witch-mount, and brake both their backs.

That autumn came King Ring north to Sogn to his wedding, and there at a noble feast drank his bridal with Ingibiorg.

"Whence came that goodly ring which thou hast on thine arm?" said King Ring to Ingibiorg.

She said her father had owned it, but he answered and said:

"Nay, for Frithiof s gift it is: so take it off thine arm straightway; for no gold shalt thou lack whenas thou comest to Elfhome."

So she gave the ring to King Helgi's wife, and bade her give it to Frithiof when he came back.

Then King Ring wended home with his wife, and loved her with exceeding great love.

CHAPTER IX.
Frithiof brings the Tribute to the Kings.

The spring after these things Frithiof departed from the Orkneys and Earl Angantyr in all good liking; and Hallward went with Frithiof.

But when they came to Norway they heard tell of the burning of Frithiof's stead.

So when he was gotten to Foreness, Frithiof said: "Black is my house waxen now; no friends have been at work here." And he sang withal:

> "Frank and free,
>
> With my father dead,
>
> In Foreness old
>
> We drank aforetime.
>
> Now my abode
>
> Behold I burned;
>
> For many ill deeds
>
> The kings must I pay."

Then he sought rede of his men what was to be done; but they bade him look to it: then he said that the scat must first be paid out of hand. So they rowed over the Firth to Sowstrand; and there they heard that the kings were gone to Baldur's Meads to sacrifice to the gods; so Frithiof and Biorn went up thither, and bade Hallward and Asmund break up meanwhile all ships, both great and small, that were anigh; and they did so. Then went Frithiof and his fellow to the door at Baldur's Meads, and Frithiof would go in. Biorn bade him fare warily, since he must needs go in alone; but Frithiof charged him to abide without, and keep watch; and he sang a stave:

> "All alone go I
>
> Unto the stead;
>
> No folk I need
>
> For the finding of kings;
>
> But cast ye the fire

>O'er the kings' dwellingly
>
>If I come not again
>
>In the cool of the even."

"Ah," said Biorn, "a goodly singing!"

Then went Frithiof in, and saw but few folk in the Hall of the Goddesses; there were the kings at their blood-offering, sitting a-drinking; a fire was there on the floor, and the wives of the kings sat thereby, a-warming the gods, while others anointed them, and wiped them with napkins.

So Frithiof went up to King Helgi and said: "Have here thy scat!"

And therewith he heaved up the purse wherein was the silver, and drave it on to the face of the king; whereby were two of his teeth knocked out, and he fell down stunned in his high seat; but Halfdan got hold of him, so that he fell not into the fire. Then sang Frithiof:

>"Have here thy scat,
>
>High lord of the warriors!
>
>Heed that and thy teeth,
>
>Lest all tumble about thee!
>
>Lo the silver abideth
>
>At the bight of this bag here,
>
>That Biorn and I
>
>Betwixt us have borne thee."

Now there were but few folk in the chamber, because the drinking was in another place; so Frithiof went out straightway along the floor, and beheld therewith that goodly ring of his on the arm of Helgi's wife as she warmed Baldur at the fire; so he took hold of the ring, but it was fast to her arm, and he dragged her by it over the pavement toward the door, and Baldur fell from her into the fire; then Halfdan's wife caught hastily at Baldur, whereby the god that she was warming fell likewise into the fire, and the fire caught both the gods, for they had been anointed, and ran up thence into the roof, so that the house was all ablaze: but Frithiof got the ring to him ere he came out. So then Biorn asked him what had come of his going in there; but Frithiof held up the ring and sang a stave:

> "The heavy purse smote Helgi
> Hard 'midst his scoundrel's visage:
> Lowly bowed Halfdan's brother,
> Fell bundling 'mid the high seat;
> There Baldur fell a-burning.
> But first my bright ring gat I.
> Fast from the roaring fire
> I dragged the bent crone forward."

Men say that Frithiof cast a firebrand up on to the roof, so that the hall was all ablaze, and therewith sang a stave:

> "Down stride we toward the sea-strand,
> And strong deeds set a-going,
> For now the blue flame bickers
> Amidst of Baldur's Meadow."

And therewith they went down to the sea.

CHAPTER X.
Frithiof made an Outlaw.

But as soon as King Helgi had come to himself he bade follow after Frithiof speedily, and slay them all, him and his fellows: "A man of forfeit life, who spareth no Place of Peace!"

So they blew the gathering for the kings' men, and when they came out to the hall they saw that it was afire; so King Halfdan went thereto with some of the folk, but King Helgi followed after Frithiof and his men, who were by then gotten a-shipboard and were lying on their oars.

Now King Helgi and his men find that all the ships are scuttled, and they have to turn back to shore, and have lost some men: then waxed King Helgi so wroth that he grew mad, and he bent his bow, and laid an arrow on the string, and drew at Frithiof so mightily that the bow brake asunder in the midst.

But when Frithiof saw that, then he gat him to the two bow oars of Ellidi, and laid so hard on them that they both brake, and with that he sang a stave:

> "Young Ingibiorg
>
> Kissed I aforetime,
>
> Kissed Beli's daughter
>
> In Baldur's Meadow.
>
> So shall the oars
>
> Of Ellidi
>
> Break both together
>
> As Helgi's bow breaks."

Then the land-wind ran down the firth and they hoisted sail and sailed; but Frithiof bade them look to it that they might have no long abiding there. And so withal they sailed out of the Sognfirth, and Frithiof sang:

> "Sail we away from Sogn,
>
> E'en as we sailed aforetime,
>
> When flared the fire all over

The house that was my fathers'.

Now is the bale a-burning

Amidst of Baldur's Meadow:

But wend I as a wild-wolf,

Well wot I they have sworn it."

"What shall we turn to now, foster-brother?" said Biorn.

"I may not abide here in Norway," said Frithiof: "I will learn the ways of warriors, and sail a-warring."

So they searched the isles and out-skerries the summer long, and gathered thereby riches and renown; but in autumn tide they made for the Orkneys, and Angantyr gave them good welcome, and they abode there through the winter-tide.

But when Frithiof was gone from Norway the kings held a Thing, whereat was Frithiof made an outlaw throughout their realm: they took his lands to them, moreover, and King Halfdan took up his abode at Foreness, and built up again all Baldur's Meadow, though it was long ere the fire was slaked there. This misliked King Helgi most, that the gods were all burned up, and great was the cost or ever Baldur's Meadow was built anew fully equal to its first estate.

So King Helgi abode still at Sowstrand.

CHAPTER XI.
Frithiof fareth to see King Ring and Ingibiorg.

Frithiof waxed ever in riches and renown whithersoever he went: evil men he slew, and grimly strong-thieves, but husbandmen and chapmen he let abide in peace; and now was he called anew Frithiof the Bold; he had gotten to him by now a great company well arrayed, and was become exceeding wealthy of chattels.

But when Frithiof had been three winters a-warring he sailed west, and made the Wick; then he said that he would go a-land: "But ye shall fare a-warring without me this winter; for I begin to weary of warfare, and would fain go to the Uplands, and get speech of King Ring: but hither shall ye come to meet me in the summer, and I will be here the first day of summer."

Biorn said: "This counsel is naught wise, though thou must needs rule; rather would I that we fare north to Sogn, and slay both those kings, Helgi and Halfdan."

"It is all naught," said Frithiof; "I must needs go see King Ring and Ingibiorg."

Says Biorn: "Loth am I hereto that thou shouldst risk thyself alone in his hands; for this Ring is a wise man and of great kin, though he be somewhat old."

But Frithiof said he would have his own way: "And thou, Biorn, shalt be captain of our company meanwhile."

So they did as he bade, and Frithiof fared to the Uplands in the autumn, for he desired sore to look upon the love of King Ring and Ingibiorg. But or ever he came there he did on him, over his clothes, a great cloak all shaggy; two staves he had in his hand, and a mask over his face, and he made as if he were exceeding old.

So he met certain herdsmen, and, going heavily, he asked them: "Whence are ye?" They answered and said: "We are of Streitaland, whereas the king dwelleth."

Quoth the carle: "Is King Ring a mighty king, then?"

They answered: "Thou lookest to us old enough to have cunning to know what manner of man is King Ring in all wise."

The carle said that he had heeded salt-boiling more than the ways of kings; and therewith he goes up to the king's house.

So when the day was well worn he came into the hall, blinking about as a dotard, and took an outward place, pulling his hood over him to hide his visage.

Then spake King Ring to Ingibiorg: "There is come into the hall a man far bigger than other men."

The queen answered: "That is no such great tidings here."

But the king spake to a serving-man who stood before the board, and said: "Go thou, and ask yon cowled man who he is, whence he cometh, and of what kin he is."

So the lad ran down the hall to the new-comer and said: "What art thou called, thou man? Where wert thou last night? Of what kin art thou?"

Said the cowled man: "Quick come thy questions, good fellow! but hast thou skill to understand if I shall tell thee hereof?"

"Yea, certes," said the lad.

"Well," said the cowl-bearer, "Thief is my name, with Wolf was I last night, and in Grief-ham was I reared."

Then ran the lad back to the king, and told him the answer of the new-comer.

"Well told, lad," said the king; "but for that land of Grief-ham, I know it well: it may well be that the man is of no light heart, and yet a wise man shall he be, and of great worth I account him."

Said the queen: "A marvellous fashion of thine, that thou must needs talk so freely with every carle that cometh hither! Yea, what is the worth of him, then?"

"That wottest thou no clearer than I," said the king; "but I see that he thinketh more than he talketh, and is peering all about him."

Therewith the king sent a man after him, and so the cowl-bearer went up before the king, going somewhat bent, and greeted him in a low voice. Then said the king: "What art thou called, thou big man?"

And the cowl-bearer answered and sang:

> "Peace-thief they called me
>
> On the prow with the Vikings;
>
> But War-thief whenas

I set widows a-weeping;

Spear-thief when I

Sent forth the barbed shafts;

Battle-thief when I

Burst forth on the king;

Hel-thief when I

Tossed up the small babies:

Isle-thief when I

In the outer isles harried;

Slaws-thief when I

Sat aloft over men:

Yet since have I drifted

With salt-boiling carls,

Needy of help

'Ere hither I came."

Said the king: "Thou hast gotten thy name of Thief from many a matter, then; but where wert thou last night, and what is thy home?"

The cowl-bearer said: "In Grief-ham I grew up; but heart drave me hither, and home have I nowhere."

The king said: "Maybe indeed that thou hast been nourished in Grief-ham a certain while; yet also maybe that thou wert born in a place of peace. But in the wild-wood must thou have lain last night, for no goodman dwelleth anigh named Wolf; but whereas thou sayest thou hast no home, so is it, that thou belike deemest thy home nought, because of thy heart that drave thee hither."

Then spake Ingibiorg: "Go, Thief, get thee to some other harbour, or in to the guest-hall."

"Nay," said the king, "I am old enow to know how to marshal guests; so do off thy cowl, new-comer, and sit down on my other hand."

"Yea, old, and over old," said the queen, "when thou settest staff-carles by thy side."

"Nay, lord, it beseemeth not," said Thief; "better it were as the queen sayeth. I have been more used to boiling salt than sitting beside lords."

"Do thou my will," said the king, "for I will rule this time."

So Thief cast his cowl from him, and was clad thereunder in a dark blue kirtle; on his arm, moreover, was the goodly gold ring, and a thick silver belt was round about him, with a great purse on it, and therein silver pennies glittering; a sword was girt to his side, and he had a great fur hood on his head, for his eyes were bleared, and his face all wrinkled.

"Ah! now we fare better, say I," quoth the king; "but do thou, queen, give him a goodly mantle, well shapen for him."

"Thou shalt rule, my lord," said the queen; "but in small account do I hold this Thief of thine."

So then he gat a good mantle over him, and sat down in the high-seat beside the king.

The queen waxed red as blood when she saw the goodly ring, yet would she give him never a word; but the king was exceeding blithe with him and said: "A goodly ring hast thou on thine arm there; thou must have boiled salt long enough to get it."

Says he, "That is all the heritage of my father."

"Ah!" says the king, "maybe thou hast more than that; well, few salt-boiling carles are thy peers, I deem, unless eld is deep in mine eyes now."

So Thief was there through the winter amid good entertainment, and well accounted of by all men; he was bounteous of his wealth, and joyous with all men: the queen held but little converse with him; but the king and he were ever blithe together.

CHAPTER XII. Frithiof saves the King and Queen on the Ice.

The tale tells that on a time King Ring and the queen, and a great company, would go to a feast. So the king spake to Thief: "Wilt thou fare with us, or abide at home?"

He said he had liefer go; and the king said: "Then am I the more content."

So they went on their ways, and had to cross a certain frozen water. Then said Thief: "I deem this ice untrustworthy; meseemeth ye fare unwarily."

Quoth the king: "It is often shown how heedful in thine heart thou wilt be to us."

So a little after the ice broke in beneath them, and Thief ran thereto, and dragged the wain to him, with all that was therein; and the king and the queen both sat in the same: so Thief drew it all up on to the ice, with the horses that were yoked to the wain.

Then spake King Ring: "Right well drawn, Thief! Frithiof the Bold himself would have drawn no stronger had he been here; doughty followers are such as thou!"

So they came to the feast, and there is nought to tell thereof, and the king went back again with seemly gifts.

CHAPTER XIII.
The King sleeps before Frithiof.

Now weareth away the mid-winter, and when spring cometh, the weather groweth fair, the wood bloometh, the grass groweth, and ships may glide betwixt land and land. So on a day the king says to his folk: "I will that ye come with us for our disport out into the woods, that we may look upon the fairness of the earth."

So did they, and went flock-meal with the king into the woods; but so it befell, that the king and Frithiof were gotten alone together afar from other men, and the king said he was heavy, and would fain sleep. Then said Thief: "Get thee home, then, lord, for it better beseemeth men of high estate to lie at home than abroad."

"Nay," said the king, "so will I not do." And he laid him down therewith, and slept fast, snoring loud.

Thief sat close by him, and presently drew his sword from his sheath and cast it far away from him.

A little while after the king woke up, and said: "Was it not so, Frithiof, that a many things came into thy mind e'en now? But well hast thou dealt with them, and great honour shalt thou have of me. Lo, now, I knew thee straightway that first evening thou earnest into our hall: now nowise speedily shalt thou depart from us; and somewhat great abideth thee."

Said Frithiof: "Lord king, thou hast done to me well, and in friendly wise; but yet must I get me gone soon, because my company cometh speedily to meet me, as I have given them charge to do."

So then they rode home from the wood, and the king's folk came flocking to him, and home they fared to the hall and drank joyously; and it was made known to all folk that Frithiof the Bold had been abiding there through the winter-tide.

CHAPTER XIV.
King Ring's Gift to Frithiof.

Early of a morning-tide one smote on the door of that hall, wherein slept the king and queen, and many others: then the king asked who it was that called at the hall door; and so he who was without said: "Here am I, Frithiof; and I am arrayed for my departure."

Then was the door opened, and Frithiof came in, and sang a stave:

> "Have great thanks for the guesting
>
> Thou gavest with all bounty;
>
> Dight fully for wayfaring
>
> Is the feeder of the eagle;
>
> But, Ingidiorg, I mind thee
>
> While yet on earth we tarry;
>
> Live gloriously! I give thee
>
> This gift for many kisses."

And therewith he cast the goodly ring towards Ingibiorg, and bade her take it.

The king smiled at this stave of his, and said: "Yea, forsooth, she hath more thanks for thy winter quarters than I; yet hath she not been more friendly to thee than I."

Then sent the king his serving-folk to fetch victuals and drink, and saith that they must eat and drink before Frithiof departed. "So arise, queen, and be joyful!" But she said she was loth to fall a-feasting so early.

"Nay, we will eat all together," said King Ring; and they did so.

But when they had drank a while King Ring spake: "I would that thou abide here, Frithiof; for my sons are but children and I am old, and unmeet for the warding of my realm, if any should bring war against it." Frithiof said: "Speedily must I be gone, lord." And he sang:

> "Oh, live, King Ring,
>
> Both long and hale!

> The highest king
> Neath heaven's skirt!
> Ward well, O king,
> Thy wife and land,
> For Ingibiorg now
> Never more shall I meet."

Then quoth King Ring:

> "Fare not away,
> O Frithiof, thus,
> With downcast heart,
> O dearest of chieftains!
> For now will I give thee
> For all thy good gifts,
> Far better things
> Than thou wottest thyself."

And again he sang:

> "To Frithiof the famous
> My fair wife I give,
> And all things therewith
> That are unto me."

Then Frithiof took up the word and sang:

> "Nay, how from thine hands
> These gifts may I have,
> But if thou hast fared
> By the last way of fate."

The king said: "I would not give thee this, but that I deem it will soon be so, for I sicken now. But of all men I would that thou shouldst have the joy of this; for thou art the crown of all Norway. The name of king will I give thee also; and all this, because Ingibiorg's brethren would begrudge thee any honour; and would be slower in getting thee a wife than I am."

Said Frithiof: "Have all thanks, lord, for thy goodwill beyond that I looked for! but I will have no higher dignity than to be called earl."

Then King Ring gave Frithiof rule over all his realm in due wise, and the name of earl therewith; and Frithiof was to rule it until such time as the sons of King Ring were of age to rule their own realm. So King Ring lay sick a little while, and then died; and great mourning was made for him; then was there a mound cast over him, and much wealth laid therein, according to his bidding.

Thereafter Frithiof made a noble feast, whereunto his folk came; and thereat was drunken at one and the same time the heritage feast after King Ring, and the bridal of Frithiof and Ingibiorg.

After these things Frithiof abode in his realm, and was deemed therein a most noble man; he and Ingibiorg had many children.

CHAPTER XV.
Frithiof King in Sogn.

Now those kings of Sogn, the brethren of Ingibiorg, heard these tidings, how that Frithiof had gotten a king's rule in Ringrealm, and had wedded Ingibiorg their sister. Then says Helgi to Halfdan, his brother, that unheard of it was, and a deed over-bold, that a mere hersir's son should have her to wife: and so thereat they gather together a mighty army, and go their ways therewith to Ringrealm, with the mind to slay Frithiof, and lay all his realm under them.

But when Frithiof was ware of this, he gathered folk, and spake to the queen moreover: "New war is come upon our realm; and now, in whatso wise the dealings go, fain am I that thy ways to me grow no colder."

She said: "In such wise have matters gone that I must needs let thee be the highest."

Now was Biorn come from the east to help Frithiof; so they fared to the fight, and it befell, as ever erst, that Frithiof was the foremost in the peril: King Helgi and he came to handy-blows, and there he slew King Helgi.

Then bade Frithiof raise up the Shield of Peace, and the battle was stayed; and therewith he cried to King Halfdan: "Two choices are in thine hands now, either that thou give up all to my will, or else gettest thou thy bane like thy brother; for now may men see that mine is the better part."

So Halfdan chose to lay himself and his realm under Frithiof's sway; and so now Frithiof became ruler over Sogn-folk, and Halfdan was to be Hersir in Sogn and pay Frithiof tribute, while Frithiof ruled Ringrealm. So Frithiof had the name of King of Sogn-folk from the time that he gave up Ringrealm to the sons of King Ring, and thereafter he won Hordaland also. He and Ingibiorg had two sons, called Gunnthiof and Hunthiof, men of might, both of them.

AND SO HERE ENDETH THE STORY OF FRITHIOF THE BOLD.

Milton Keynes UK
Ingram Content Group UK Ltd.
UKHW020825231024
450026UK00004B/396

9 789362 922779